APPLETREE PRESS

GW00631064

a hand scribed selection of
IRISH TRADITIONAL DISHES

JOHN MURPHY

CALLIGRAPHY BY MARGARET BATT

Published by
Appletree Press
19-21 Alfred Street
Belfast BT2 8DL

The Pick of Irish Recipes
A catalogue record for this book is available
from the British Library.

ISBN 0-86281-607-6

9 8 7 6 5 4 3 2 1

Printed in Ireland

Preface

These recipes have been collected from various sources. Many were collected from friends and relations who, in the nature of things, had them from their mothers and their mothers before them. Others were culled from such dusty volumes as The Complete Confectioner or the Whole Art of Confectionery Made Plain and Easy by H Glasse (Dublin, 1742) and The Lady's Assistant for Regulating and Supplying Her Table by Charlotte Mason (Dublin, 1778).

The recipes themselves cover the country, from Donegal pie and yellow man in the north to drisheen from Cork, taking in on the way gur cake and coddle from Dublin and baked ham from Limerick. I hope you enjoy cooking and eating these dishes as much as I have collecting them.

boxty in the pan

1 tsp. salt
1 lb. flour
1 tsp. baking soda
1 lb. raw potatoes
1 lb. mashed potatoes
buttermilk

Peel the raw potatoes & grate them onto a linen teatowel. Squeeze and collect the liquid in a basin, & leave to stand. Mix the grated potatoes & the mashed potatoes. When the starch has separated from the liquid pour off the water and add the starch to the potatoes. Add the dry ingredients and mix well, then add enough buttermilk to form a dropping consistency. Beat well & leave to stand a little before frying in spoonfuls in a greased pan. Fry on both sides & serve with butter & sugar.

5

barm brack

salt
2 eggs
1 lb. flour
2 oz. butter
½ lb. sultanas
½ lb. currants
¾ oz. yeast
½ pt. milk [warmed]
2 tblsp. sugar
4 oz. mixed peel
ground cinnamon
grated nutmeg

Sift the flour together with the spices and a pinch of salt, then rub in the butter. Cream the yeast with half the sugar and a little milk. Mix the rest of the sugar into the flour, add the warmed milk, eggs & yeast, and beat well. Fold in the fruit and the mixed peel. Turn into an eight inch buttered cake *(over)* tin, cover with a cloth and leave in a warm place to rise for about an hour, or until it has doubled in size. brush the top with a little beaten egg. bake near the top of a hot oven for one hour. ∿∿∿∿∿∿∿∿∿∿∿

boxty on the griddle

1 tsp. salt
¼ lb. flour
1 lb. raw potatoes
1 lb. mashed potatoes

Proceed as for 'boxty in the pan' adding enough flour to make a workable dough. knead a little, then roll out and cut into farls. bake on a hot griddle & serve warm with butter.

tripe and onions

1 pt. milk
1 lb. tripe
chopped parsley
1 lb. onions
1 oz. flour &
1 oz. butter
blended together

Cut the tripe into two inch squares bring to the boil three times in fresh water. slice the onions. add the tripe & the milk. season and simmer over a low fire for about two hours. Thicken the liquid with the flour and butter. add seasoning and serve sprinkled with parsley.

Cockle Soup

parsley
stick of celery
1 oz. flour
1 oz. butter
1 quart cockles
1 pt. water
1 pt. milk

COVER the cockles with cold water and boil until they open. Shell them, removing the beards, & keep the liquor. Make a roux with the flour and butter. Blend in the liquor and the milk, add the chopped celery and simmer for half an hour. Return the cockles, & add the chopped parsley. Cook gently for a few minutes. Serve

Yellow Man

1 lb. syrup
¼ lb. butter
1 lb. brown sugar
1 tsp. baking soda
2 tsp. vinegar

Dissolve the sugar, butter, syrup and vinegar, then boil without stirring until a drop hardens in cold water. Remove from the heat and quickly stir in the soda which will foam up. Pour into a greased tin to cool & break into chunks. Store in an airtight tin

Willicks

Sea Water
1 pt. willicks or winkles

Cover the willicks with sea water. Boil for ten minutes. Eat with a pin when cool. ❧

Take the fish, scale, remove the head, fins, and gut them. Wash & pat dry, then toss in seasoned flour. Fry rapidly on both sides until the skin is crisp. Continue frying for a further five minutes or until cooked. ❧

Herrings
salt & pepper
flour

Fried herrings

Carrigeen Moss Blancmange

lemon rind
1½ pt. milk
2 tblsp. sugar
½ oz. carrigeen moss

Wash the moss. Place in a saucepan with milk and lemon rind. Bring slowly to the boil & add the sugar. Strain into a wetted mould. Turn out when set and serve with stewed fruit.

brotchán foltchep

parsley
2 lb. leeks
2 pt. milk
knob of butter
2 oz. oatmeal
salt & pepper

Boil the milk with the oatmeal until cooked. Add the butter and mix in the chopped leeks. ⁂
Cool gently for one hour. Season to taste & garnish with chopped parsley. ⁂

a pot of tea

water
milk
good quality tea
sugar

Bring freshly drawn water to the boil in a kettle. Use a little to warm a 1½ pt. earthenware teapot. Empty the pot, then add 3-4 teaspoons of good tea. Bring the kettle back to the boil. Pour the boiling water into the pot, then stir once. Cover the teapot with a cosy and let it brew for five minutes. Serve with milk & sugar.

guinness cake

4 eggs
1 lb. flour
1 lb. sugar
1½ lb. dried fruit
1 tsp. baking soda
½ lb. butter
¼ lb. cherries
¼ lb. mixed peel
¼ lb. almonds
pinch nutmeg
1 bottle guinness
1 lemon

Rub the butter into the flour. mix well with the dry ingredients. add the guinness, lemon juice & beaten eggs. bake in an 8 inch tin in a slow oven for about three hours.

buttermilk pancakes

1 egg
1 lb. flour
1 tsp. baking soda
large pinch of salt
1 pt. buttermilk
2 oz. sugar

Mix the dry ingredients. Add the egg & enough buttermilk to make a batter of a dropping ⁕ ⁕ ⁕ consistency. Fry in spoonfuls on a hot greased ⁕ ⁕ griddle. Serve warm with butter and jam for tea. ⁕

Drisheen

2 pt. milk
1 pt. water
2 pt. sheep's blood
¼ lb. breadcrumbs
1 lb. mutton suet
2 tsp. salt

Strain the blood and mix with all the other ingredients in a basin allow to stand for one hour. Cover well & simmer for about three quarters of an hour. Cut into pieces and serve hot.

donegal pie

½ lb. bacon
2 hardboiled eggs
2 lb. mashed potatoes
½ lb. pastry

Grease a pie dish & half fill it with potatoes. Slice the eggs & place on top. Fry the bacon until crisp, then place on top of the eggs and pour over the bacon fat. Cover with the rest of the potatoes. Make a pastry lid and bake in a hot oven for about one & a half hours. Serve. ✤ ✤ ✤

bookie's sandwich

butter
2 lb. steak
1 long crusty loaf
mustard

slice the loaf length-
wise and butter.
it. Fry the steak & place
on one half of the loaf. ❧
Spread with mustard and
season to taste. Replace
the lid and allow to cool
under a light weight. Cut
into slices when cool. keep
wrapped until ready to eat.

SCONES

1 egg
½ lb. FLOUR
¼ pt. milk
large pinch salt
1 tsp. baking powder
2 oz. SUGAR
¼ lb. butter

Sieve the flour, baking powder and salt. Rub in the butter & mix in the sugar. beat egg & milk together. add to form a loose dough & knead lightly, flattening out to about half an inch thick. Cut into scones with a round cutter. bake at the top of a hot oven for about fifteen minutes. Serve hot for preference.

black caps

½ lb. sugar
18 pippins
2 tblsp. orange flower water
juice & rind of a lemon

halve the apples. ·:· Set them together, cut side down, in a dish. Pour the lemon juice, rind and orange flower water over the apples. Sprinkle with sugar, and bake in a moderate oven for half an hour.

baked salmon

parsley
1/4 lb. butter
1 whole salmon
1/2 pt. cream
salt & pepper

Clean the salmon & rub with butter. Place in a dish, pour the cream & chopped parsley over it, then season lightly. Cover & bake in a moderate oven (allow ten minutes per lb.) baste a few times.

mince pies

7 lb. suet
3 lb. sirloin of beef
7 lb. currants
2 lb. raisins
3 oz. cinnamon, cloves & mace
grated rind & juice of a lemon
& orange mixed
6 apples
1 oz. caraway seeds
1 pt. white wine
2 lb. sugar
pastry

STEEP the caraway seeds overnight in white wine. mix with all the other ingredients, having minced the beef, shredded the suet & chopped the apples. bake in pastry, made in the usual way in a moderately hot oven for about half an hour.

apple jelly

4 lb. sugar
a dozen cloves
4 lb. water
4 or 5 lb. apples
(good windfalls will do)

Wash the apples, and cut coarsely. Place in a crock with the cloves and cover with the water. place in the bottom of a very low oven & leave overnight. Strain the liquid through a jelly bag without squeezing. measure the liquid and add 1 lb. of sugar for each pint. dissolve the sugar and boil until the liquid gels when tested on a cold saucer. store in clean dry jam jars ❧ ❧ ❧

Gur Cake

1 egg
2 oz. milk
2 oz. flour
½ lb. stale bread or cake
½ tsp. baking powder
2 tsp. mixed spice
pinch of salt
½ lb. currants
2 oz. brown sugar
knob of butter
½ lb. pastry

Grate the bread or cake & soak the crumbs in water for an hour, then squeeze out. Mix with the dry ingredients & combine with the egg (beaten) & milk. Roll out the pastry, cut in two & line the base of a 9 inch sq. tin. Spread the mixture evenly on top, and cover with the rest of the pastry. Bake for an hour & a half in a moderately hot oven. When ready (over)

remove from the oven and
sprinkle with sugar. Allow
to cool and cut in squares.

apple tart

water
1 tsp. salt
6 oz. butter
2 lb. cooking apples
12 oz. flour
4 oz. sugar

Sieve the flour and salt
and rub in the butter,
mix to a pliable dough with
a little water, then allow to
rest in a cold place while
peeling & slicing the apples.
Roll out the pastry and line
an 8 inch buttered pie-dish.
Fill with apple slices and
sugar, & cover with pastry
lid. Cut a vent in the top,
seal the edges & bake near
the top of a moderately hot
oven for a little over half
an hour. Serve hot or cold
with cream.

baked limerick ham

cloves
brown sugar
bread crumbs
water to cover
10/12 lb. centre cut ham

Soak the ham overnight. place in a pot cover with water and bring to the boil. Simmer on a low fire (allow approx. twenty mins. per lb.) Remove from the pot & strip the skin. press a mixture of breadcrumbs & brown sugar onto the fat. Insert the cloves. bake in a moderate oven for three quarters of an hour

Pig's Head Brawn

mace
cloves
mixed herbs
peppercorns
2 onions
1 small pig's head & tongue
2 pig's feet

CLEAVE the head in two, remove the eyes, & brains and any gristle. Wash well & scrape where necessary. ❖ ❖ Scrub the feet well. Just cover the meat with water in a pot &, add the herbs & spices Simmer for six hours over a low fire or until the meat is very tender. Remove the meat from the bones & return to the pot and keep boiling to reduce the liquid. Remove the (over)

28

skin from the tongue and
slice. Fill a tin mould with
the pieces of meat, packing
well while still hot. If too
dry add a little stock from
the pot. Allow to cool with
a weighted plate on top.
When cold turn out & slice.

hot whiskey

2 cloves
1 tsp. sugar
1 measure of whiskey
1 slice of lemon

WARM a stemmed
whiskey
glass with very hot water.
Pour in boiling water and
sugar to taste. Stir to
dissolve the sugar, add a
good measure of whiskey, a
slice of lemon & some cloves.

nettle broth

scallions
2 lb. boiling beef
2 pts. nettle tops
a cup of barley
salt & pepper

cut up the meat. place it with the barley in a pot, and cover it with half a gallon of water. Simmer over a low fire for two hours. Add the chopped nettles and scallions, and cook for a further hour. Season to taste.

black pudding

intestines
small onion
½ lb. oatmeal
½ gal. pig's blood
½ lb. bread crumbs
½ lb. pork belly chopped
salt & pepper

Wash the intestines well & soak in salt water overnight. Mix the ingredients together & stuff into the intestines. Form into rings and tie each end. Place in a pot, cover with water and cook over a low fire for about two hours. Eat cold; or cut in slices and fry, and serve with fried bacon and eggs.

CRUBIN

water
pickled pig's feet

Allow two pig's feet per person. Cover with water & bring slowly to the boil. Simmer over a slow fire for three hours, or until the meat is tender. Serve hot with soda bread.

❁ ❁ ❁

Soak the beans overnight. Cook the feet and split open. Allow them to cool & coat in egg & breadcrumbs. Dot with butter & grill, cooking the beans at the same time. Serve hot.

dried white beans
egg & breadcrumbs
butter
pickled pig's feet

CRUBIN SUPPER

Irish Stew

1 pt. water
1 lb. onions
2 lb. potatoes
2 lb. breast of mutton
or gigot chops
salt & pepper

Trim the meat & place in the bottom of a stewing pan, add some sliced potatoes and onion, season with salt and pepper, and add the water. Bring to the boil & simmer for about an hour. Add the remaining sliced potatoes & onions, cover & simmer for a further hour. When cooked, serve on a hot dish with the potatoes & onion surrounding the meat—

Stirabout

1 tsp. salt
3 oz. oatmeal
2 pts. water

bring the water to boil & sprinkle on the oatmeal. add the salt. Simmer gently on a low fire for two hours. Serve with honey, butter or milk

Mix the oatmeal with the salt & hot water form into large flat cakes. Cook on a moderate griddle on one side until firm arrange around the fire until dry on the upper side.

hot water
1 lb. oatmeal
salt

Oatcakes

potato apple

apples
4 oz. flour
1 lb. potatoes
½ tsp. salt
1 oz.. butter

boil the potatoes, &
mash well, mak-
ing sure there
are no lumps. mix in the
flour and knead to make a
pliable dough, but not too
much as this will toughen
it. Roll out into a circle
cut the apples into thick
slices & place on one half.
fold the other half on top
& pinch round to seal. cook
on both sides on a griddle,
until the apples are cooked
slice around, peel back the
top & add lumps of butter
& sugar. keep hot by the
fire until the butter & the
sugar have combined.
serve in slices.

boiled brisket

1 carrot
1 large onion
1 small turnip
2 oz. barley
3 lb. boiled brisket
salt & pepper

Place the meat in a pot, cover with boiling water and add the barley. Simmer on a low fire for one & a half hours. Cut the vegetables coarsely and add to the meat. Continue cooking until tender. Serve the meat on a dish, with the vegetables arranged around it.

stewed eels

eels
white sauce
parsley

Skin and clean the eels, then cut into three inch pieces. place in a pot, cover with cold water and bring to the boil. simmer for five minutes, and then drain. add a pint of white sauce. stew for three quarters of an hour add the chopped parsley serve

mutton broth

1 onion
2 carrots
2 leeks
small turnip
1 tblsp. barley
1 lb. lean neck of mutton
parsley
salt & pepper

Cut up the meat. Dice the vegetables. Simmer over a low fire in one & a half pints of water for about two hours. Serve hot.

champ

scallions
½ pt. milk
5 lb. potatoes
butter
salt & pepper

boil the potatoes

and mash well. chop the
scallions and heat with the
milk, then beat into the
potatoes with a wooden
spoon. season and serve
hot, with a large knob of
butter in the centre of each
plateful. eat from the out-
side in, dipping each forkful
into the melted butter

Dublin Coddle

1 lb. onions
3 lb. potatoes
1 lb. best pork sausages
2 lb. thick slices of streaky
or back bacon
parsley
½ pt. water or stock

Cut the bacon into two inch square pieces · boil, together with the sausages for five minutes, then place in a dish. Cover with thickly-sliced potatoes, the onions and the water or stock. · Sprinkle with parsley & cook in a moderate oven, or simmer on top of the stove for an hour.

Potato Farls

4 oz. flour
1 oz. butter
1 lb. potatoes
½ tsp. salt

Boil the potatoes. Mash well, making sure there are no lumps. Mix in the flour and knead until it is elastic enough to roll out, but not too much as this will toughen it. Roll out into a circle & cut into four farls. Bake until brown on both sides on a hot dry griddle or strong frying pan. Best eaten with two fried eggs and several rashers of good bacon

boiled bacon and cabbage

1 cabbage
2 lb. piece boiling bacon
water

Place the bacon in a saucepan. Cover with water and bring to the boil. Simmer for about two hours, or until tender. Remove the bacon, slice the cabbage and add to the water. boil for about ten minutes, keeping the bacon warm. Slice the bacon, drain the cabbage & serve.

soda bread

1 lb. plain flour
¾ pt. buttermilk
1 tsp. bicarbonate of soda
1 tsp. salt

MIX the dry ingredients together, making sure there are no lumps in the soda. Add the buttermilk and mix well with a wooden spoon. Knead lightly on a floured board. Place on a baking sheet & mark the top with a cross. Bake at the top of a hot oven for three quarters of an hour, until the bottom of the loaf sounds hollow when rapped with the knuckle—— ∴ ∴ ∴

pratie oaten

fine oatmeal
mashed potatoes
salt

Work the oatmeal into the potatoes to make a dough. Roll and cut into farls. Cook on a hot griddle. Serve hot or cold, with plenty of butter

44

Colcannon

butter
½ lb. cabbage
3 lb. potatoes
small onion
salt & pepper

Boil the potatoes, drain, & mash well. Chop up the cooked cabbage & mix in with the potatoes. Chop the onion & cook gently in butter until soft & mix into the potatoes & cabbage. Serve on hot plates with a well of butter in the middle of each mound.

45

spiced beef

1½ lb. salt
1 oz. saltpetre
1 lb. brown sugar
(moist)
6 lb. middle rib
rolled & boned
6 tsp. mixed spices
(thyme, mixed herbs, mace
nutmeg cloves and allspice
black pepper and bay leaves)

POUND the herbs & spices together and mix well with the salt, sugar saltpetre and minced onion. take the beef, boned, rolled and tied up well, and place in an earthenware crock. Cover the meat with the spice mixture, rubbing it well in by hand for several minutes. Replace the lid. Repeat every day for a fortnight, turning the meat once a day. ❧

46

Index

Drisheen, 17
Dublin coddle, 40
Fried herrings, 11
Guinness cake, 15
Gur cake, 25
Hot whiskey, 29
Irish stew, 33
Mince pies, 23
Mutton broth, 38
Nettle broth, 30
Oatcakes, 34
Pig's head brawn, 28
Pot of tea, 14
Potato apple, 35
Potato farls, 41
Pratie oaten, 44
Scones, 20
Soda bread, 43
Spiced beef, 46
Stewed eels, 37
Stirabout, 34
Tripe and onions, 8
Willicks, 11
Yellow man, 10